Dangerous Australians

The wild animals of Australia are reputed to be some of the most dangerous and bizarre creatures in the world. Their strange bodies and even stranger lifestyles are the results of ancient and ongoing struggles to survive in a harsh and isolated land.

When it comes to eating or being eaten, Australian animals make the most of what they have. Their remarkable arsenals of protective features and survival strategies are the very reasons these animals can be a danger to people.

Very few Australian animals deliberately attack humans, but many will defend themselves with deadly skill when threatened or frightened. Being aware of how these fascinating animals live and behave can mean the difference between rewarding wildlife encounters and dangerous ones.

THE BIG BITE

The Saltwater Crocodile is one of nature's success stories. Its body plan and hunting techniques have changed little since its prehistoric ancestors preyed upon dinosaurs.

Armour-like skin, powerful muscles, acute senses and massive jaws make the crocodile a formidable predator. It is a master of the lurk and ambush school, keeping the bulk of its body submerged while zeroing in on its next meal. Using the famous death roll, a crocodile drowns large prey quickly and secures it under water for later consumption.

The Saltwater Crocodile is Australia's biggest reptilian carnivore. It inhabits the seas, shores, rivers and wetlands of northern coastal regions. Saltwater Crocodiles will eat anything they can catch, including humans, if given the opportunity.

These nocturnal hunters are particularly active during the wet season when food is plentiful and breeding occurs.

A Saltwater Crocodile lunges out of the water propelled by its powerful tail.

A lurking crocodile may be mistaken for a floating log.

A crocodile has 66 teeth, each of which may be replaced many times over during the owner's lifetime.

The average size of an adult male Saltwater Crocodile is 5 m.

SHARK ATTACK

Few creatures evoke as much fear as the Great White Shark. Armed with a gaping maw of jagged teeth, this swift and silent hunter survives in a world alien to most people.

Like other sharks, the Great White's senses are tuned to the vibrations, electrical impulses and chemical traces that animal bodies produce. They are efficient predators whose size and indiscriminate tastes place them at the top of marine food chains.

On average, one person is killed by a shark every year. Of the 166 local species, the Great White, Oceanic Whitetip, Tiger and Bull sharks have been responsible for most of these attacks.

The increasing urbanisation of the Australian coastline has created more opportunities for people and sharks to meet. In some cases developments, such as harbours and canals, have provided new habitats for sharks.

The harmless Port Jackson Shark has flat grinding teeth.

Sharks may gather in a feeding frenzy for live prey or bait.

Whitetip Reef Sharks are territorial, but are more of a nuisance than a danger.

The Great White Shark prefers cool, southern oceans, but may be found in most Australian coastal areas.

The Tiger Shark may grow to 5 m in length and has a voracious appetite.

HIDDEN DANGER

Fish leading cryptic lives on the sea floor rely on stealth and camouflage to catch prey. Their venomous spines are reserved for defence against real or perceived predators. The spines carry strong toxins that cause pain, numbness and, sometimes, death to animals as large as a human. These marine fish do not prey on humans, but do pose a danger because they are difficult to distinguish from their surrounds.

A stonefish's deadly spines can pierce rubber-soled shoes.

The Striped Catfish has three venomous spines.

A sting from a Red Rockcod produces pain and numbness.

A Common Lionfish has 13 venomous spines along its back.

The Eastern Stargazer has a venomous, grooved spine on each shoulder.

A small electric ray, the Numbfish may generate 50 shocks within 10 minutes.

The Masked Stingaree is not an electric ray. However, the spines on its tail are toxic.

SHOCK VALUE

Some rays catch food and protect themselves with electricity. Kidney-shaped organs near the head generate electrical charges as strong as 220 volts. An electric ray can give off a series of gradually weakening shocks before it has to recharge. Swimmers shocked by a ray may lose consciousness or mobility and risk drowning.

THE LAST MEAL

Humans risk being poisoned when they join marine food chains as predators of fish. Several kinds of fish have toxins in their bodies that are harmful or lethal when eaten. These poisons are not destroyed by cooking.

Some Pufferfish species are regarded as a delicacy, but the toxins that are made and stored in their skin and organs make them a risky meal. An inflatable body with prickly skin and a bad taste is the pufferfish's first line of defence against predators. Using the trial and error approach, the predators learn to recognise and avoid these fish. Those that do not learn, do not live to eat again.

Some tropical and warm-water fish consume and store toxins from the food they eat. The higher up the food chain, the greater the concentration of toxins. These toxins cause ciguatera poisoning in humans, but have no effect on the fish. Ciguatoxins are thought to originate in tiny organisms that live in seaweeds.

Parrotfish are a source of ciguatera poisoning, which causes vomiting, low blood pressure and nerve damage.

The Saddled Pufferfish advertises its dangerous nature with bright warning colours.

The toxins in the Star Pufferfish's body may cause numbness, vomiting, paralysis and death.

MISTAKEN INTENTIONS

Human curiosity and a taste for excitement can turn a marine wildlife encounter into a scarring experience. Divers and other reef visitors often hand-feed fish so they can get close to these curious and beautiful animals. However, a fish may interpret these human attempts at bonding as a threat to its safety or as competition for food.

A fish confronted with a probing finger may defend itself with a lunging mouthful of sharp teeth. Or, in its eagerness to get an easy meal, the fish may not distinguish where the food ends and the hand begins.

Fish that are used to being fed learn to associate people with food and can become very bold. When their expectations are not met, they may become annoyed or decide to see if people are also food. Some of these fish, especially cods and wrasses, have large, heavy bodies, and a tail flick or sideswipe can be painful.

A Green Moray Eel hunts for prey amongst the crevices of a rocky reef.

Moray Eels have razor-sharp teeth and should not be teased.

The Potato Cod can exceed 1.5 m in length and can weigh up to 100 kg.

THE UNTOUCHABLES

Many marine invertebrates produce strong, fast-acting toxins that are used for immobilising prey and warding off predators. They come equipped with a variety of spines, barbs and darts for injecting the venoms. The effects of these venomous bites and stings on humans may range from pain to paralysis and respiratory failure.

Fire Coral is a colony of tiny animals armed with stinging tentacles.

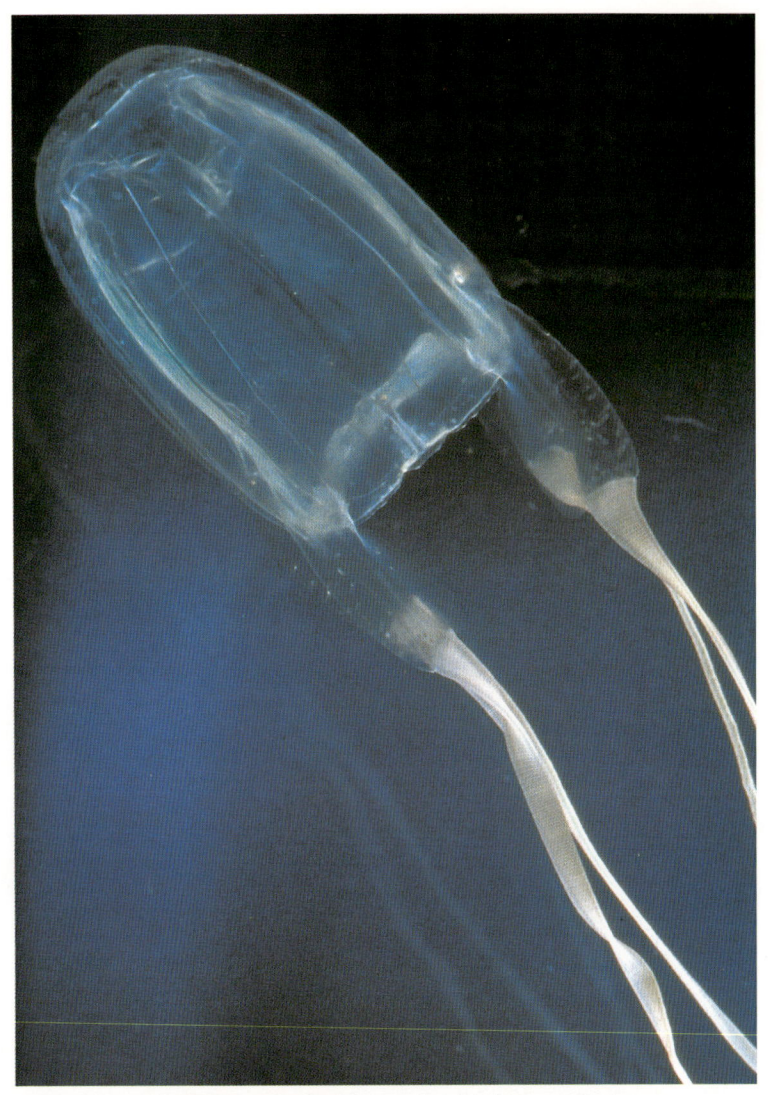

Irukandji sea jelly stings can be fatal for people with heart conditions.

A Textile Cone extends its proboscis to fire venomous darts that are loaded with toxins that affect the human nervous system.

The 4 cm–long Blue-ringed Octopus is the deadliest octopus in the world.

A fern-like colony of hydrozoans can deliver painful stings.

Needle-sharp sea-urchin spines penetrate deeply and are difficult to extract.

The 2 m long tentacles of the Box Sea Jelly contain millions of stinging cells.

WILD DOG

The Dingo is Australia's largest, carnivorous mammal. It was brought here from south-east Asia about 4000 years ago. The Dingo is a type of primitive dog, and, unlike domestic dog species, it breeds only once a year.

Dingos are opportunistic predators and mammals are their main source of food. They also prey on reptiles, birds, fish and even insects. They usually hunt alone, but will form a pack to bring down large animals.

Dingos are wild animals that normally avoid humans. In places where Dingos receive food handouts, they may lose their fear of humans and come to regard them as weaker animals. A bold Dingo may bite the hand that tries to feed or stroke it. A fearless one may stalk and attack people. To date, there have been confirmed fatal attacks by Dingos.

Although sporting less common colouring, this black and tan Dingo is a purebred and should not be mistaken for a domestic dog.

The Dingo's forward pointing ears are alert to the sounds of prey.

Waterholes attract Dingos and their prey.

The Dingo has longer canine teeth than domestic dogs of the same size, and uses these teeth to bring down and eat its prey.

A Dingo eats its kill.

DEADLY FANGS

Australia is home to over 380 species of land snakes. Less than 30 of these are potentially dangerous to humans.

All snakes are carnivores, although their energy-efficient bodies require little food. These cold-blooded reptiles spend most of their time moving in and out of the shade to regulate their body temperature. A snake's flexible skeleton gives it great agility, but its metabolism allows only short bursts of speed.

Snakes make good use of camouflage colours, acute senses and a hinged jaw with recurved teeth to overcome the challenges of being limbless. Venomous snakes have the added advantage of fangs and toxic saliva. Venom quickly subdues and kills prey without energy-consuming pursuits and struggles.

Australian front-fanged snakes are renowned for their potent venom, yet the rate of human fatalities is low. Most snakes are not aggressive and will retreat if left alone. A snake will defend itself if provoked or attacked. Over 80% of bites occur when people try to catch or kill snakes.

The Northern Death Adder's bite is potentially lethal to humans.

SNAKE BITES

Front fangs
Snakes with hollow front fangs strike quickly and inject their prey with venom.

Back fangs
Rear-fanged snakes must catch and hold their prey before injecting the venom.

No fangs
Snakes without fangs and venom hold prey with their teeth and coils while they swallow it.

DEGREES OF DANGER

The danger rating of a venomous, front-fanged snake depends on:
- venom toxicity
- venom quantity
- strike rate
- fang length
- temperament

A Common Death Adder sinks its fangs into a gecko.

The Western Brown Snake is one of seven brown snake species that are responsible for the highest number of human fatalities.

The Mulga or King Brown Snake produces more venom than any other land snake.

Although it has not caused human fatalities, the Copperhead's venom damages nerves, blood cells and other tissues.

Although venomous, the rear-fanged Brown Tree Snake is not a danger to humans.

The non-venomous Carpet Python constricts prey with its coils.

The nocturnal Stephen's Banded Snake is extremely aggressive.

CHEMICAL COCKTAILS!

Different snake venoms have varying combinations of chemicals, each of which affects different parts of the victim's body.

- coagulants – cause blood clotting
- anticoagulants – prevent blood clotting
- neurotoxins – damage nerves
- myotoxins – affect muscles
- heamotoxins – break down red blood cells.

The Eastern Tiger Snake and its relatives are responsible for, on average, one fatality per year.

Eastern Tiger Snakes are highly variable in colour and not all are banded.

A bite from a Black Whip Snake can cause a painful, swollen wound.

Red-bellied Black Snake venom can be lethal to small children.

The Coastal Taipan will strike repeatedly when cornered and is highly venomous.

The Inland Taipan has the most toxic venom of any land snake.

There have been no fatalities in Australia from venomous seasnake bites.

SEA SERPENTS

Twenty-two of Australia's 33 marine snake species are considered potentially dangerous as their venom is toxic to humans. However, their short, front fangs cannot penetrate protective clothing. Most are found in the tropics.

Seasnakes have poor vision and are attracted to shiny things, such as the reflections from a diver's mask or air bubbles. A seasnake will touch an object with its head to determine whether or not it is food. This may be disconcerting for novice divers who may panic and provoke a defensive attack.

Sea kraits have a potentially fatal bite. Although partly terrestrial, they hunt under water for fish and eels. They lay eggs onshore, unlike seasnakes, who bear live young and never leave the water.

The Banded Sea Krait has a potentially fatal bite.

EIGHT-LEGGED MENACE

Spiders are enduring, if not endearing creatures. They can trace their ancestry back 360 million years. The basic, eight-legged prototype has since diversified into more than 25,000 species found throughout the world.

Spiders have developed bodies and lifestyles to suit their dual roles as predators and prey. The silk-spinners with their trip-wires and nets are just as successful as the venomous hunters at catching prey and defending themselves. All spiders have saliva that liquifies body tissue so they can suck up their food.

Several thousand species live in Australia and each kind has found a suitable niche within a varied landscape of natural and built environments. Some are considered dangerous because they are common and their venom damages the human body.

Trapdoor spiders, including the Mouse Spider, have venomous fangs.

A Sydney Funnel-web rears up ready to attack. There are 37 species of funnel-web spiders and their lethal venom attacks the human nervous system.

The bite of the female Red-back Spider can be lethal. However, there have been no fatalities since an antivenom was invented in 1956.

A bite from a Black House Spider may cause pain and vomiting, but it is not deadly to humans.

White-tailed Spiders prey on Black House Spiders. Their bite may cause ulcerating wounds and tissue necrosis.

Ticks may carry diseases harmful to humans.

The scorpion's sting may cause an allergic reaction.

ARMED LOW-LIFES

Scorpions, centipedes and ticks are small biting or stinging animals that live on or near the ground.

Scorpions are nocturnal predators that hunt other invertebrates. A scorpion holds its prey with large pincers, then delivers a paralysing sting with its tail. The sting is painful for humans and can cause an allergic reaction.

Centipedes kill insects, spiders and other small animals with their jaws and venomous saliva. Centipedes and scorpions sometimes take refuge in human belongings left on the ground. Their bite is extremely painful, but no human fatalities have been recorded in Australia.

A tick is a blood-sucking parasite. It buries its jaws in a host animal's skin, causing itchy, swollen wounds. The toxins injected by a paralysis tick's bite can paralyse and kill small animals. Ticks may be carriers of human diseases, such as Q Fever, Tick Typhus and Spotted Fever.

The centipede's bite is extremely painful.

PERILOUS SWARMS

There are an assortment of insects whose bites and stings can cause irritation, pain and, in some cases, life-threatening allergic reactions.

These six-legged animals use their venomous weapons for defence. Some ants and wasps also use venom for paralysing or killing prey to feed themselves or their young.

Most of these insects live in colonies. A combined response to threats or food opportunities means a group of these small animals can overcome prey and predators much larger than themselves.

Ants and wasps can sting repeatedly, but the introduced European Honeybee only gets one chance. When it retreats after an attack, its barbed sting is torn from its body and the bee dies.

The formic acid in Green Ant stings causes fiery pain. Ice or cold water offers relief.

The Meat Ant worker has a venomous stinger on its hind end. The sting may irritate skin and cause local swelling.

Some people are allergic to Honey Bee stings. Extreme allergic reactions may lead to death.

Depending on the victim, the effect of a Paper Wasp sting varies from brief pain to strong allergic reaction.

THE UNSEEN

Bacteria and viruses often hitch rides on or in the bodies of wild animals. These microscopic organisms are picked up in the places the animals live or in the food they eat. The hitchhikers change carriers when the animals come into contact with humans. Bacteria and viruses can cause serious diseases in humans, even though their animal carriers may show no ill effects.

Some Fruit Bats carry the Hendra virus that causes symptoms similar to pneumonia.

Bush Flies transmit bacteria that may spoil food and cause infections.

Some mosquitos carry viruses that cause dangerous diseases, such as Encephalitis, Dengue Fever and Ross River Fever.

THE UNEXPECTED

Trying to get up close and personal with some Australians can be hazardous. Many native animals are tolerant of human encroachment on their habitats, and some are quite at ease accepting handouts of food. They are not aggressive animals and would rather flee than fight.

However, in some situations animals may view human behaviour as frightening. Wild animals may cause injury with their tails, claws or teeth as they try to defend themselves or escape a threatening situation.

Monitors have powerful, clawed limbs that could inflict painful wounds.

A large male Red Kangaroo may weigh up to 85 kg.

Kangaroos such as these Eastern Greys have powerful hind legs and sharp claws.

Even tame Sulphur-crested Cockatoos will bite if teased.

The male Platypus has a venomous spur on each hind ankle.

PROTECTIVE PARENTS

Birds can be very territorial, especially during breeding season. Masked Lapwings and Australian Magpies will launch aerial attacks on anything they think is a threat to their eggs and chicks. Unsuspecting trespassers can be startled, frightened or wounded.

The Emu and Southern Cassowary are protective parents too. It is the males who incubate the eggs and care for the chicks. A kick from one of these tall, flightless birds can inflict serious injury.

Australian Magpies will attack during the breeding season, from August to October.

Masked Lapwings have a sharp spur on the front edge of each wing.

Emus have been known to grab food from picknickers.

The razor-sharp nails on a Southern Cassowary's inner toes can grow to over 12 cm long.

AMPHIBIOUS ASSAULT

Secretions from a frog's skin glands help it survive. The antifungal and antibacterial secretions protect against infection, while the poisonous ones are a defence against predators. Only some frogs have poison glands and they usually advertise their distasteful natures with bright, warning colours.

The introduced Cane Toad not only poisons native animals, it also out-competes them for food and habitat. The Cane Toad's lethal toxins act on the heart and could kill humans if the toad or its eggs are eaten.

People should not put their hands near their eyes or mouths when handling frogs and toads, and should wash their hands afterwards.

A Moaning Frog deters predators with poisonous secretions.

The Cane Toad is a deadly menace that was introduced to Australia in 1935.